# The Alphabet Not Unlike the World

Also by Katrina Vandenberg

*Atlas*
Milkweed Editions, 2004

*On Marriage*
(with Todd Boss)
Red Dragonfly Press, 2008

# The Alphabet Not Unlike the World
# Katrina Vandenberg                    Poems

milkweed
editions

Published 2012 by Milkweed Editions
Printed in the United States
Cover and interior design by Hopkins/Baumann
Cover photograph by Tony Howell
Author photo by John Reimringer
The text of this book is set in Bodoni Book with Bodoni Bold.
13 14 15 16   5 4 3 2
*First Edition*

Please turn to the back of this book for a list of the sustaining funders of
Milkweed Editions.

Library of Congress Cataloging-in-Publication Data

Vandenberg, Katrina, 1971-
   The alphabet not unlike the world : poems / Katrina Vandenberg. -- 1st ed.
      p. cm.
   Includes bibliographical references.
   ISBN 978-1-57131-446-8 (alk. paper)
   I. Title.
   PS3622.A588A79 2012
   811'.6--dc23

                              2011040886

This book is printed on acid-free paper.

A is for Anna

# Contents

Acknowledgments     VIII

Prologue: A Ghazal     2

## ᚱ

| | |
|---|---|
| Self-Portrait in 1970 | 7 |
| B | 8 |
| The Autumn Our Babysitter Was Murdered by Her Boyfriend | 9 |
| Siren Song | 10 |
| C Ghazal | 11 |
| Palinode for Adolescence | 12 |
| Hot Air Balloons over Lenox, MA | 14 |

## ◬

| | |
|---|---|
| D Ghazal | 19 |
| *Live Through This* (1994) | 20 |
| E | 21 |
| My Sister Visits Her Ex in Prison Once a Year to Ask Him Whether He Did It | 24 |
| *Courage and horror stand side by side* | 25 |
| Say something | 27 |
| Once, he had brain fever | 29 |
| Saint Kevin's Bed | 31 |
| Poem on Tim's Thirty-Fifth Birthday | 32 |
| The Monks' Fishing Hut | 33 |
| Bearing Witness | 34 |
| *Cell* | 37 |
| N | 38 |
| Winged Monkeys | 40 |
| Cretaceous Moth Trapped in Amber *(Lament in Two Voices)* | 42 |

## ι

| | |
|---|---|
| Connemara | 47 |
|    1. On the Bog Road | |
|    2. Fuchsia | |
| Making Her Black Bean Chili Again | 49 |
| Detroit | 50 |
| The Night the Painter Unpinned Her Hair | 51 |
| We Kept Having to Say | 52 |
| Abyss | 53 |
| On Marriage | 54 |
| K | 55 |

## Ϟ

| | |
|---|---|
| She thinks of herself as a green Dodge van | 58 |
| Oarlock, Oar *(Y, W, V, U, F)* | 60 |
| Handwriting Analysis | 62 |
| Photograph: My Parents' First Christmas | 63 |
| Mirror Palace | 64 |
| Virginity | 66 |
| By Now the Warning Bell Has Rung and None of Us Can Drive | 67 |
| Transparent | 69 |

## ⊗

| | |
|---|---|
| M | 73 |
| O, P, R, S (Eye/Mouth/Head/Tongue) | 75 |
| Q | 76 |
| I think of myself as the old borrowed bicycle | 79 |
| Earthworms | 80 |
| X | 81 |
| Plums | 82 |
| Z Ghazal | 84 |
| | |
| Notes | 87 |

# Acknowledgments

I would like to thank the editors of the following magazines in which some of these poems first appeared, sometimes in different forms:

*Arkansas Literary Forum:* "Detroit" (as "Dinner with Ex-Lover, Ten Years Out")
*Blackbird:* "D Ghazal," "Once, he had brain fever" (as "Dark Ages")
*Cave Wall:* "*Live Through This* (1994)," "My Sister Visits Her Ex in Prison Once a Year to Ask Him Whether He Did It," "The Autumn Our Babysitter Was Murdered by Her Boyfriend" (as "Poem for the Cave Wall")
*Connotation Press, An Online Artifact:* "B," "C Ghazal," "E," "N," and "Hot Air Balloons over Lenox, MA"
*Dislocate:* "Bearing Witness," "The Monks' Fishing Hut," "Poem on Tim's Thirty-Fifth Birthday," "Saint Kevin's Bed"
*Ecotone:* "On Marriage"
*Linebreak*: "*Courage and horror stand side by side,*" "Virginity"
*Memorious*: "Abyss," "The Night the Painter Unpinned Her Hair"
*Orion*: "Fuchsia," "Earthworms," "O, P, R, S (Eye/Mouth/Head/Tongue)" (as "Driving to Hilary and Doug's Cabin in Northern Wisconsin")
*PoetLore*: "Siren Song"
*Post Road*: "Cretaceous Moth Trapped in Amber *(Lament in Two Voices),*" "Palinode for Adolescence"
*The Rumpus:* "Say something"
*The Southern Review:* "A Ghazal," "X," "Oarlock, Oar *(Y, W, V, U, F),*" "Z Ghazal"
*The Sun:* "We Kept Having to Say" (as "One Argument for the Existence of God")
*Third Coast:* "Mirror Palace"
*Waccamaw:* "By Now the Warning Bell Has Rung and None of Us Can Drive" (as "Birth Order"), "Handwriting Analysis"

Many of these poems were written with the support of a Bush Artist Fellowship, a Loft-McKnight Award, and an artist initiative grant from the Minnesota State Arts Board. Many of these poems were written at the MacDowell Colony; the Poetry Center of Chicago; and the Amy Clampitt House near Lenox, MA. Many of these poems were revised at the Sewanee Writers' Conference, thanks to a Tennessee Williams Scholarship. I am grateful to all of these foundations and organizations, and the kind and inspiring people associated with them, for their gifts of money, time, and believing.

The poems "On Marriage," "We Kept Having to Say" (as "Why Some People Want to Believe There Is No God"), "On the Bog Road," (as "On the Bog Road to Connemara"), and "Making Her Black Bean Chili Again" were either published or reprinted in the limited-edition fine-arts chapbook *On Marriage*, co-authored with Todd Boss (Red Dragonfly Press, 2008). "We Kept Having to Say" also appeared on *Flurry* and was reprinted in the 2012 Syracuse Cultural Workers' *Women Artists Datebook*. "On the Bog Road" was anthologized in *Perfect Dragonfly*, ed. Scott King, Red Dragonfly Press, 2011.

"She thinks of herself as a green Dodge van" was read at the inaugural Great Twin Cities Poetry Read on April 30, 2010, and anthologized in *Poetry City, U.S.A.*, Vol. 1, ed. Matthew Mauch, Lowbrow Press, 2011.

"Say something" was reprinted in *The Rumpus Original Poetry Anthology*, ed. Brian Spears, 2011.

"Plums" first appeared in a different form in the anthology *Visiting Dr. Williams: Poems Inspired by the Life and Work of William Carlos Williams*, ed. Thom Tammaro, University of Iowa Press, 2011.

"A Ghazal," "Cretaceous Moth Trapped in Amber *(Lament in Two Voices),*" "M," and "Photograph: My Parents' First Christmas" were either published or reprinted in *Fire On Her Tongue: An eBook Anthology of Contemporary Women's Poetry* eds. Kelli Russell Agodon and Annette Spaulding-Convy, Two Sylvias Press, 2011.

Thanks to the Twin Cities literary community, especially Daniel Slager and the staff of Milkweed Editions; editors Jim Cihlar and Wayne Miller; poet-friends and readers Deborah Keenan and Anna Meek; and my colleagues, students, and friends at Hamline University, the Loft Literary Center, and Micawber's Books.

For making me feel welcome in the Berkshires, where I spent six months away from home writing much of this book, thanks especially to poets Karen Chase, Hannah Fries, and Leslie Harrison; painter Paul Graubard; Matt Tannenbaum of The Bookstore in Lenox; Chip Blake and the staff of *Orion;* and the late Amy Clampitt and Harold Korn, for use of their home and big dictionary, which got me started on the alphabet poems.

Thanks to my mother, who surrounded me with books; my father, who taught me how to use a dictionary; my sister, who let me read to her years past the point we knew it should stop; and John, to whom I owe my happiness and Baby Anna. The two of which might be the same thing.

The Alphabet Not Unlike the World

## Prologue: A Ghazal

The Phoenician A is 𐤀, *aleph*. The ox points its nose forward. A
is strong enough to pull the train of letters through the poem. A.

See the yoke clutch its neck. Is the poet driving? No,
it's the man who hewed the yoke leading the ox to market, to heap A

with what he needs to get through winter. He is sending the letters
on a long drive through the early snow. What will burden A

before it can return to the barn? *A* for *alpha, most important*
—an *alpha* dog, a compelling man. A lucid star, o scarlet letter *A*

for *spontaneous abortion,* the early miscarriage's true name.
The doctor adds, "It's nothing you did," even if it does start with A,

not your fault, this bloody end to a beginning. Squeezes your hand
each time. In the beginning was the apple, round and red. A,

"Apple of my eye," your father used to say, A for the round red
embryonic sac. *Aardappel,* Dutch for *potato,* starts with A—

*ground apple, aard* meaning *earth,* sounds like *hard,* it's a hard
world sometimes, hard-packed under oxen feet, and A

for *aardvark,* too, for *absence, abstain, absinthe.* ⤚ sleeps
on its side in the straw. In one Nordbrandt poem I like, "A,"

"Already in the word's first letter / the word already is there /
and in the word already, the whole sentence . / . . . / as the a-

lmond tree is in each almond / and a whole almond grove in the tree…"
Already in the beginning was the Word, the letter A,

gold stars, *almonds,* you can have *another, asshole, and,*
*alienate.* "Apple of my eye," your father said, twinkling A,

that dangles from its stem, that cannot last, that gets one booted
from the garden every time. What bears fruit this time of year? "A,"

insists Nordbrandt: "… already in the word's first letter / the almond
trees are in bloom." Saith the Lord, "I am the Alpha and the Omega."

Saith Katrina, "Already the pure child and all the unborn inside it
have been forgotten with the path the ox broke through the snow: ⤚."

# Self-Portrait in 1970

The Phoenician symbol 𐤐 *papyrus* drops from the alphabet

without a word why does it go when I stay

dividing          I who arrived on a starry river

thunder in the distance                    the papyrus reeds

in the swamp of the Nile delta they could be

bowls be paper woven into sails mats braided

into the cords Odysseus uses to bind the door

before he slays the suitors  in her body all of the sperm

had to die but one I am bloody umbilical already the man

and the woman are rearranging furniture

                                        I am

waiting for fingers on which to count the ways

of papyrus it could be woven into a shallow basket

to carry me downriver to them

home for the unwritten

city of Byblos city of books the alphabet empty paper

boats the burned-out stars the continuous unscrolling

list of the dead all becomings fall away but one

# B

Old as the Egyptians, as the need for a way in or out,
be strong, my house, like the ox, and never move. B
is for *beth*, ᗺ, as in *Bethlehem*, the house of bread,
and *Bethel*, House of God. *Bethany* is a house
made of trees sagging with dates and mercy.
There is the house that the psychologist asks
the boy to draw, to see whether the floors
are being swept inside his body.
The boy is careful, but forgets to draw the door.
B is for *beta*, it's only a test: how much resilience
does he have? Why do people suffer?
The houses made of figs and gleaming fish,
they laugh. They say, *Because.*

## The Autumn Our Babysitter Was Murdered by Her Boyfriend

the neighborhood mothers leaned their heads together

over a jug of Gallo an ashtray a soap opera

said *Never think love changes anyone*

then told my sister and me *Go back outside*

to the homemade playhouse its shutters from our real house

its proportions crazy all fall she and I obsessed

about storms knocking off shingles tossing in

fistfuls of apple leaves into November

the women talked my mother scolding

*Never think love changes anyone* we made

the beds made families from knives forks plates

my sister and I obsessed about stopping the wind

from blowing off the playhouse's Dutch door

first its top half then its bottom

the untold story shifted the wind took the door

both halves along with the leaves

I have a sister we wanted to stop the wind

*Nevernever* our mother said *does love change anyone*

## Siren Song

Even now, when I remember
        the first times I could hear it,
I bow my head as I did then

—as if in prayer, as if
        I were a horse testing
for slack in my reins.

All of us girls could hear it.
        We could not stop,
the cross-legged row of us

who braided each others' hair
        during fourth-grade story hour.
The librarian's *Girls,*

*this is not a beauty parlor!*
        could not hold up against
the solemn whisper from

behind, *Let me play with*
        *your hair*; against
the anonymous fingers

that grazed your nape,
        gathering even before
you nodded *yes*. The tune

was pitched so we alone
        could hear: *Keep*
*plaiting*. We plaited

loose ladders that soon
        might bring men to us,
men who might get us out.

# C Ghazal

⌐ is *gimel* or *camel*, a work-beast ruminant with one hump.
Good children learn that water sloshes in the wine-skin of its hump.

The boy's cigarette package: three palms and a pyramid, bound
in cellophane. A camel in the middle with its furry, saddled hump.

It no longer matters whether you were a teenager who smoked
in a wooded place dubbed Egypt. *What the camel keeps inside its hump.*

Charm-sized camels on each cylinder. His Zippo lighter. An orange star
glows, burns each camel to ash. Another secret lost inside each hump.

The Magi's camels *galled, sore-footed, lying down in the melting snow.*
A hard time you had of it. Talk about now: do you ride the camel's hump,

or are you being ridden? Everyone is blowing smoke, telling tales
of misspent youth. The package bears the shadow of the hump.

What is your burden? What didn't you choose? Do you stumble as beast
or as king? Before what wheeling compass of stars? You're over the hump,

it's done. C for the things Katrina carries toward the horizon's starry hump.
C for the wobbly desert cadence, the awkward sustenance within the hump.

## Palinode for Adolescence

Let me take it all back: last summer
I did not crouch with a group of college students
on a pilgrimage, under a tomb
in Saint Brigid's cathedral in Kildare

to see a hidden stone carving of a sheela-na-gig, naked
and parting her legs to show her gaping vulva.
The students were a careless sort,
not inclined to take notes. The boys were not

uncomfortable. One did not mock-moan,
"Oh, Sheela, Sheela!" as he rubbed his knees
and righted himself. No, none of it was as I said.
At their age I did not make love with a boy

with HIV for the first time, not
believing that if a condom broke, I could die.
Ask my mother: she will tell you
I have a flair for the dramatic. I am sorry

I misled you about the carving's moronic grin,
the black hole of her womb, her fierce
and glinting eyes. The students did not buy
Cadbury bars and Orangina whenever

the tour bus stopped. They tended
toward the dour, crying and eating apples.
The cathedral does not have a pit in which Brigid's nuns
tended her fire for a thousand years, sacred

in a land of rocks and rain. Brigid's fire
still burns. Actually, it is the students
who are a thousand years old and remember
Brigid with her crosier, the good old days

in her schoolyard when they played with fire
and found life sweet, took notes in French class
on how their phrase for *orgasm* means *little death*,
that feeling of falling someone might learn

under another body and like it so much
she would not give it up, whatever the danger.
Finally, none of the students were beautiful. When
the girls' jeans rode low enough that you could see

their incandescent skin, their gluteal clefts
would not have reminded you of peaches.
I did not remember what it was like to be
their age while under a tomb, on my knees.

## Hot Air Balloons over Lenox, MA

*When you were sixteen, you knocked*
          *on a door* — the balloons:
                    cartoon thought bubbles

out of reach. How slow their waft,
          how high the huff of fire. Red,
                    yellow, nearly suspended, your

high-school girlfriend's earrings,
          the set of windchimes in
                    my mother's maple, silent

now. Good weather in which to be
          aloft. Parachute spiders
                    hook one strand of silk

on the wind — how delicate
          the gondola's wicker weave,
                    how easy to miss

from the ground their procession
          with the clouds. When you were sixteen,

you asked to crew — two hungover
          summers of wielding fans
                    and flames to inflate, deflate,

though most of the work was chasing, scouting
          for fields without power lines
                    where the balloon could land.

I was six, then, a girl handed
          balloons on strings and sticks,
                    a girl always watching

the sky. How peaceful the ride,
       they say, the envelope
              shaped like an inverted tear,

an inverted jug of wine. When you
       were sixteen, you knocked on
              a door — how peaceful

the ride through death is said
       to be. Whitman says he stops
              somewhere waiting for me. Where?

Nothing stays. Look, look up —
       not currents of air, the rising
              heat, the floating moon. Maybe

we learn to untether from
       the earth. Some days the balloon man
              took you up. The view

scrolled underneath: planned patchwork
       of Kansas prairie, endless
              wheat undulating

over mammoth bones asleep
       in the bed of a former warm
              inland sea — how slow

is geologic time, how elegant
       the web, infinitely slower than
              balloons overhead, than your

twenty years of chasing, coming to find me.

# D Ghazal

Let D kick things off as it would in the Book of Kells, gold-leafed D.
Vine-wrapped D. Lions and ravens strut around its Royal D-Ness. *D.*

Down the street children color in its middle when it shows up
in the chapter book, with O's and R's. Already doors left unopened.

*D* sounds like a door, slammed.
Case closed.

The sound of *de,*
                    beginning a word, is that word's undoing.
At its end, *De-*'s evil twin *-Ed* says the word is dead.

In the Phoenician alphabet it is ◢, *daleth*, a crude door.
They packed it with purple dye and glass in a cargo hold,

sailed it to the Greeks, who wrote it Δ for *delta*,
the river's maw. In chemistry Δ accuses, "You've changed."

And so it is written, Δ, Δ, Δ for years. Slips of white paper
folded into warm cookies. Your fortune tongue-tied inside.

As in *Deliberate, Dust, Dinosaur*. As in *Donkey, Doo-hickey, Don't.*
D, the metal shoe with which the other letters' horses are shod.

Do you still hear them stampede into the future,
Dopplegänger, shadow boy? Each year it is your death I hold

against the light of November, to ask myself how I have done.
I give myself a ◢, the door that faces backward.

Would you even know me?—Katrina, pure amber that trapped
your boyhood self. These days, I'm a hurricane. These days, a flood.

# *Live Through This* (1994)

Everywhere it was tribe on tribe, wars in countries she could not have named, mass rape, genocide. At home brutality was shot with glitter. O. J. Simpson outran the dead blonde in his Bronco; Susan Smith released her Mazda's brake, her dozing babies into the lake. The Bobbitts — but it's my mother watching the news. My sister is twenty-one and unmarried,

all ripped jeans and flannel, soaping her baby in the kitchen sink. She covers her daughter's eyes, pours a cup of water over her head to rinse, whispering, *Look up at the man in the moon.* Tiny flowered pj's and a soft song, *ER* with my mother until my sister's friend honks and she runs into the driveway to see Courtney Love at Joe Louis Arena, to finally light a Camel and rummage through broken jewel cases on the floor, to moan about Kurt Cobain,

and though she's in it, she doesn't like the beer- and sweat-soaked jostling in the pit, strange boys who grab at the breasts she's still using to nurse, so when a boy asks, "Do you want to get out?" she nods, misunderstanding — he hoists her up; her body begins to surf over the waving lighters, the bobbing heads. And Courtney Love, smeared lipstick, dress open to show her bra, looks down to meet her terrified eyes. Pulls her up onto the piano bench. Continues her song. 1994,

and the white Bronco outruns trouble, the army boots stamp, the lighters wink like stars that burn out before their light reaches earth, in the great gaping mouth of the Joe — and my sister perched above the mob, glad her baby sleeps through this, a curled soft fist under a plugged-in plastic star. Sleeps through Courtney in her ripped babydoll dress, who struts and screams *Go on, take everything.*

# E

Once, a man with his arms raised to the sky was part
of the alphabet.

Some days we are comfortable enough that we don't know the sky
is there at all, much less that we should raise our arms to it.

I think that many still privately raise their arms to the sky.
And more would, if their arms would remind them to say
*yes* or *no* or *help us*.

E is the most common written letter in my language.

In Kilkenny, Saint Fiacre knelt in his garden, raised his arms
toward the balloon animals of the shifting clouds. Then he pulled
leeks from the ground and ferried them off in baskets. Honey,
beeswax, medicinal herbs.

E is Energy, and energy is matter, in the famous equation that,
for maybe twenty seconds, satisfied us all; e is electrons buzzing
around a center, frantic planets around a sun, bees and an
emptied hive.

Behind the razor wire in Jackson, Michigan, among the men in
orange jumpsuits, my sister's ex Michael must want to raise his
arms to the sky, though he probably doesn't. There, raising one's
arms to the sky means *Don't shoot*.

So much space exists between electrons that every object in the
world is mostly empty. And most of what our eyes perceive is just
light and edges.

Prisoners and saints: men in cells.

In math, the backwards E, $\exists$, means *there exists*. $\in$ means *part of a set*. A line through that $\notin$ means *excluded from*. Everyone $\exists$, but not everyone $\in$. We all feel that, unless we $\in$, we do not $\exists$.

The coroner says Michael punched his live-in girlfriend's child in the stomach many times. Michael says he did no such thing. Everywhere, there are different ways of dying.

It is terrible to remember that night, and with only a poor handful of letters, hard to explain.

A fly on the wall has 4000 lenses in each eye, a 360-degree view, a quick sense of the swatter, and poor vision.

Sky is space; you cannot hold the blue. Reach high as you will, and you will never touch it.

It's been five years. No one visits but his mother. He will never come out, no matter what.

Fiacre, it is said, barred women from his monastery, threatening any who scaled its garden walls with severe bodily pain.

Michael works in the prison garden now, it is said, helping to grow their food.

Tomatoes are part of the nightshade family, and were decorative plants in Thomas Jefferson's garden, because people feared they were poisonous.

Fiacre is the patron saint of gardens and florists, also French taxicab drivers and STDs.

The calmest we ever saw Michael was at my sister's side when she was giving birth.

Why am I telling you? Because there are large spaces between the things I understand.

I think that people are not evil, but are afraid.

I think you want to raise your arms to the sky.

The tomato is not the sky. It is pulpy and red, with star-shaped stems, prone to cat scratches and bruises. The sky is your face holding its breath. Sky is a trick of the eye.

A *Why-is-the-sky-blue?* question is a childish one without an answer, except that there is an answer, and it is scattered light.

The night sky is black and encrusted with moths.

The first man, we say, lived in a garden and tried to be good. But there were all these tomato vines unfurling around his feet, and fruit proved to be his undoing.

**My Sister Visits Her Ex in Prison Once a Year**
**to Ask Him Whether He Did It**

She goes alone, tells no one she is going, always
the night before Easter, when the altar
is stripped, black veil draped over the cross.
The same night my sister and I, when we were girls
and mistaken for twins, dyed eggs, dissolving
colored tablets in glasses of vinegar.

Two years ago when she asked him whether
he killed the little boy, he said *I can't tell you*
*for the life of me.* Last year, no answer.

### *Courage and horror stand side by side*

say the gods who

               dole out fates. Like        the one they give

      the massage therapist

raped              in her office     by a

     stranger off the street.
               Raped face-down

on her table, in              dimness and

      lavender oil. *No,*      *this is yours,* say

the gods,
handing off

        a profusion of fall days    in Boston, when
                         the boy you loved
                         was dying. Each morning

on your way to see him      you cut a bouquet

of cosmos from
the front steps of
a brownstone.
          The other, *not yours,*
                   is braver than yours, how
                       it ends—

the therapist feared she would die

hating him and began to chant,

and the panicked rapist             ran, not knowing

she was chanting the
Buddhist prayer
for compassion.

*And did you sing for your enemies?*

No.

The gods are busy.

The cosmos are lavender,

rose, tangled and

orange,

replacing themselves in what

seems hours.

## Say something

about the old neighbor who lives alone, the woman
no one has seen in years, if at all. Say she cracked

her yellowed shade and spoke to you, soon after
you moved in, mid-winter. *Change the locks*,

she said. A gray fox lived
in our city neighborhood. Say *foxes*, say

this one slinked over her fence at night, leaving
a trail of prints in the snow. Say *The woman*

*set out a bowl of milk*, say she shooed you away
when you tried to shovel snow from her walk,

fetch her a sack of lightbulbs and eggs. What I am
saying is, I knew a woman, she lived near me

in the house of the unsaid, its refrigerator powered
by an antique pull cord, live wires lashing within

her walls—that her tub was clawfoot; the trim,
black walnut. In paint-peeled closets

were headless torsos she once dressed, and
pinking shears, fawn-colored scraps of velveteen.

In that dried gourd she rattled, rattled.
When moon-suited firemen climbed inside,

the upstairs window was singing with flies.
Death bled into the unfinished dresses—

what I am saying is, no one could find
a walker, a garbage can, her purse, or her keys.

I am saying — she would agree — The way
the pattern is fitted against the bolt of cloth

matters before you are done. We worry, now
who moves in? The house festers, it swells;

she turned inside it, unable to say how
it became unmanageable, why

she hid notes in the drawers, addressed
To the Man Who Steals My Electricity.

## Once, he had brain fever

I stayed at the hospital all night. All night
        he wanted water, wanted to pour
                the glass himself, and though

his hands unsteadily flapped
        I kept handing over the pitcher.
                I had no answer

when the night nurse,
        on her third time out the door,
                arms loaded with soaked sheets,

hissed, *Why do you keep letting him?*
        None of us matters to the future.
                The monk whose breath

blown through a hollow reed
        sealed gold leaf to gesso
                on a page of the Book of Kells

has otherwise left no trace.
        He could not read the words
                he copied out, yet labored

over his share for decades.
        What if each night is one
                illuminated page? Then

see the cup, the straw; the glaze
        of water on the swinging table
                becomes a Celtic spiral

of lapis lazuli. See the nurse
      — a lion — who stalks
            the margins (she's tinted

vermilion) of a psalm you know
      by heart, the one in which
            your cup runs over.

## Saint Kevin's Bed
### —*Glendalough*

And this is where he stayed awake, praying
and hungry; this cave, the tomb of a Bronze Age king
is where all night he asked for mercy, on his knees
where, once, the king's bones moldered and his gold

for the next world was plundered. Opposite
Kevin hung the moon — an empty mirror,
the taut skin on a bodhrán he could not hear.
He chanted from this cliff above the treetops

and the mica-schist his cave was made of
flaked away around him; the monster
he had yet to fight flexed in the lake below.
I came alone to Glendalough. Within a day

a group of college students on a pilgrimage
picked me up, and their guide told Kevin's story
as we looked at his cave from the cliff's far side.
We never went in: you need a boat, the cliff

erodes, the cave is fragile — just big enough
for one to lie in, which is why they say
no one, not even a saint, could live there long,
that dark hole in the past no one can get to anymore.

## Poem on Tim's Thirty-Fifth Birthday
### *(July 28, 1969 - November 20, 1994)*

You would know me
if you saw me— still Lucille Ball
on the candy factory line, swallowing
the proof that I can't keep up. I married,
the way you asked. Other changes
you'd be less happy about: your records gone,
the CD collection frozen at '94. Chip said
Uncle Tupelo turned into someone else
years ago; I never noticed. Think
of all the dancing we did not do. I could
use a new song. Let's call this your last
poem for now. But what does one do instead
with the remains? All this time
I've written from this desk to those I love
and never told—that your ashes are inside it,
in a Ziploc that is starting to break down.
You must be on my paper clips, this page,
my thank-you notes. You must be in my mouth
and in my blood. In that way, nothing's changed:
I'm losing you. Even the box of this poem
won't be enough.

## The Monks' Fishing Hut
### *— Cong Abbey*

Back when their kitchen
was charged with feeding
thousands, the monks built

a stone fishing house over
the flood — cut a trapdoor
in the floor, lowered

a wooden cage into the
water, hitched a small bell
to its rope. When salmon

washed in, current-trapped,
the bell would ring, and
the monks knew, once again,

they would be fed. I still
consider our hunger
to hold on to the dead —

the tail-thrash of a memory
taken whole — but the dead
are gone forever. Like you,

whom I came all this way
to the ruins of a fishing hut
to catch. Like the girl I was

back when you wrote me
a love letter from
the nearby footbridge

where I now stand
listening to the river
press on and on.

## Bearing Witness

Saint Kevin did not see the bird

                         coming, his arms

outstretched as he knelt

                             in prayer

above the lake in a beehive cell

                             so narrow

he held

                   one arm out the window. Later

they said

                   *blackbird*, they said *Holy*

*Ghost*, but the angle blocked his view.

                        He just let her rest

in his upturned palm, until,

                         weeks later,

the warm eggs shivered.

                         Who knew

he could hold his arm that still,

                         that long?

He was not holy;

                         he was

a hermit, and human.

                         I know this

story will not help you

                              on the day you take

the stand
                    in a polka-dotted dress,

eleven, and
                              the only witness

to the night
                              your father hit

your four-year-old stepbrother
                                        until

he was dead. Stick
                              to your blurry story
                    he did not

do it he was on the other side
                    of the bathroom door giving

the boy a bath, Luke cried
                    all the time. Let the green

speckled shells of *oath* and *truth*
                              be broken
                              in time from
                              within. For now

the judge will take you
                              from the courtroom
                    before the lawyers show

autopsy slides,
                    and I want you to take

Kevin's story and hold it

                      perhaps for years.

He, too, could not see

                the long task coming —

the lives

                we find unexpectedly

in our hands.

# Cell

comes from *celare, small room*, cousin to the word *conceal*. Also brother to *helare*, or *hell*.

Hell is holding on to a secret, some of us already know.

*Keep the cough drop in your cheek so you don't choke*, her mother says.

The word comes to the body from the private room for prayer — beehive huts in which Irish monks sat, copying manuscripts. The monks netted stories like fish, tossing nothing back.

She copies from the blackboard: *cell = smallest unit in the body, the building block of life.*

She is eleven, scraping a toothpick against the inside of her cheek, floating one lens on the other to make the wet-mount slide.

*Semi-permeable membrane*, she writes. *Colonies function as organs, systems.*

She squints into the microscope. *Draw and label it neatly by ten of the hour.*

Probably she is an A student.

*Is there anything else you'd like to share with the class?*

# N

There's the fear of tight spaces of bridges of spiders of clowns

water mirrors the dark though really they're all the fear of living

on a highwire alone the fear of heights Philippe Petit dances

with his pole between memory's towers again there sweats

my palms my soles every caver I've met is claustrophobic that's why

they squirm in to the rock's tight mouth carbide lamps bandaged

to their foreheads squeeze through chinks within the typeface

you must enter the thing you're afraid of

you must offer it something to eat the hieroglyph of a snake

is *nahs* the letter N in Arabic *nahs* means *bad luck*

the Phoenicians turned the N into *nun* the fish no one

has ever believed the dead are friendly all our gestures

the gauze-draped mirror the open window the veil

the brooch made from hair are meant to make the dead

go quietly there's fear of death of snakes our neighbor's lost boa

lived in our house God knows how long when I was small

there's fear of places from which escape might be difficult

we never saw it my father found behind the water heater

its shed skin a scroll in a language none of us could read

there's fear of public speaking fear of squeezing the snake's

markings millions of years in the making the moist world

the hibiscus vine calling the snake forth the constricting

on each exhale until the breaths can out no more you break

snap bone you suffocate you must go in the house

as for the boa I imagine it wove itself

across the kitchen linoleum into the bath hissed

back into the sewer one night drained under the street

in the house of childhood you cannot stop your ears

when the neighbor girl tells you how tapeworms

are called from the body you only need to

be hungry hold out a bowl of milk open your mouth

## Winged Monkeys

As I might have said to Trevor, *A stage hand got caught in some cables,*
*fell from a tree and hanged himself during the filming of*
*The Wizard of Oz, and they never cut or re-shot the scene.* See
for yourself, in the background in a red shirt a dead man swings

as the Scarecrow and Dorothy and the Tin Man link arms, chirping
of what they're off to. I'd look it up to make sure, but I want to tell you
as if you're my friend, we're in grad school and at Arsaga's for coffee
or something, hungover and shooting the shit, complaining

we've no time to *work* when really, our days fall open wide.
We're splitting a bagel. It's okay if I'm wrong. The hanged
man in the red shirt: a juicy apple; a lantern swung
in the railyard by a gandy dancer like my great-uncle, sliced in half

by a train in the early days of the Rock Island Line. What happened
is they stop in the forest to pick apples, the witch wings a fireball,
the Scarecrow's chest catches fire. How do they put it out?
Who needs to know, all's well that ends well, they skip deeper

into the trees and into darkness. How many times did you answer
that question on a Shakespeare test, *What does the forest symbolize?*
*Change* and *being lost* got you credit, as did *transformation, internal*
*confusion.* The *Prelapsarian World* was always a nice touch.

Trevor thought I said one of the winged monkeys (little minions,
scarier than the witch, just human enough) was strangled by a pulley.
He and his boyfriend rewound the tape *like a hundred times*, he said,
scanning the flock for disaster. When the boyfriend broke it off

three days before he moved to Brooklyn, Trevor accused me of saying,
once, that I understood how it was, to be gay. *And how could you? How*
*could you?* he said. Early Sunday morning, no one out, we're on the steps
of the art center downtown, and I can't remember what he's referring to

but say I'm sorry anyway. I am. Whatever it was, I probably did say it,
asserting sureness in the ways of the world, the way I did. The way I do.
Probably there are people, all kinds of people, so deep in the frame
I miss them, or it's easier not to see them, since I can't do it over anyway.

## Cretaceous Moth Trapped in Amber *(Lament in Two Voices)*


What a shame I have nothing to give you but midnight, my story
*Little moth caught forever in the last moment of before,*

of five French soldiers with identically shaved heads,
*when the dusk was thick with incense and crickets*

the one who spit in my hair, the one who slapped me,
*and great northern evergreens wept puddles of resin*

the one who kissed my mouth as the others watched.
*on the forest floor. What were you stammering toward*

Their green nylon jackets, their laced boots, their laughter,
*the night you got stuck, a moon lost in thought*

the glass wall of the lit phone booth they pushed me against.
*as it cast its glistening net over tree frogs, over the mites*

I got away. But when I reached my unlit street
*punctuating the laddered webs of orb weavers,*

and they were still following me, I had to choose:
*over the orb weavers about to be lodged in resin*

break for the host family's door? Or light back
          *themselves? This is the story now under glass,*

to the phone booth, to the main drag, where
          *honeyed and see-through: a palm of red-gold*

yellow headlights kept slipping by? I wanted
          *beads traded for swords and furs in the Viking town*

home. I chose the glass box, though I feared it a trap.
          *of Dublin. And in millions of years*

I moved toward the lights.
          *the moon has not changed; it is still perched*

Today I know that saved my life.
          *in its starry web, dropping its sticky strands.*

But you know what I am saying, moth.
          *The world has not changed; there is still a great deal*

It could have just as easily been different.
          *of getting caught in it, you must choose.*

L

## Connemara

### 1. On the Bog Road

And it was that summer fear for the marriage
arrived in search of me. I don't know where
it came from, from ten thousand years
of heavy rainfall, its continual beat
against the rotting flowers to make peat.
It did not come from skylark or meadow
pipit, butterwort or mountain sorrel, not
the turf banks, not the occasional pony
munching tufts of moorgrass
but in the bogs one afternoon I was summoned
in wet Gore-Tex and muddy jeans.
There I was without you, and fear
slid his ringed hand from his cassock and he touched me.

I did not know what to say, my mouth dumb
before the landscape and its history
of the orphan boys who wet their beds
and were made to run all night by priests
through their stone schoolyard with soiled bedsheets
over their heads, to make them dry.
I followed the waver of the moths,
took my first footstep off the road
into the bog, watched the water rise to meet my boot,

and the boys broke loose
from their unmarked graves and wheeled
through the bens with white sheets over their heads,
and the bog gave back all it had held onto
these thousands of years — cauldrons, rings, holy
books, wagon wheels — for I
had become part of the vast lake
made by sixty-three inches of rain a year
times ten thousand in Connemara.

## 2. Fuchsia

That summer in the west I walked sunrise
to dusk, narrow twisted highways without shoulders,
low stone walls on both sides. Hedgerows
of fuchsia hemmed me in, the tropical plant
now wild, centuries after nobles imported it
for their gardens. I was unafraid,
did not cross to the outsides of curves, did not
look behind me for what might be coming.
For weeks in counties Kerry and Cork, I walked
through the red blooms the Irish call
the Tears of God, blazing from the brush
like lanterns. Who would have thought
a warm current touching the shore
of that stone-cold country could make
lemon trees, bananas, and palms not just take,
but thrive? Wild as the jungles they came from,
where boas flexed around their trunks —
like my other brushes with miracles,
the men who love you back, how they come
to you, gorgeous and invasive, improbable,
hemming you in. And you walk that road
blazing, some days not even afraid to die.

## Making Her Black Bean Chili Again

There's a book of recipes I want to collect, working title *Recipes from the Ex.*
Every woman has one. You've got to dish it out the way he likes it sometimes.

Because a marriage has got to feed its ghosts, or they'll never let you be.

I hear his was five feet tall like me, but strong enough to stand her ground
on a hiking trail spraying bear bomb at a mother grizzly as she charged.

Clearly a woman you should listen to. So I keep making it the way she says.

I drink a glass of Rioja while I'm cooking, listen to my favorite Cole Porter on CD,
liking his dissonant chords beneath the chipper words. It was just one of
   those things.

Dice the tomatoes, add lime juice, garlic, red pepper flakes, cayenne.
  Green chiles. Stir

until once again from spicy steam and blackness she's been conjured—Julie,
packing heat and spraying pepper all over the part of the trail she never traveled.

## Detroit

So here we are — white tablecloth and a window,
the sweat of our water glasses, shy twirl of noodles

against a spoon. His body, ten years later, now
thickened into a stranger's. I hear, in the heart

of my old hometown, Detroit, some buildings
and blocks have been abandoned so long, wildness

is coming back to the city. I hear men
have begun to stalk pheasants again in the vines.

## The Night the Painter Unpinned Her Hair

A pool game was going in the artist colony's main hall,
someone had built a fire in the fireplace, it had
begun to rain. There was the clack, the strike
and the painter unpinned her hair. She
and the composer sat on the sofa, stiff, not looking
at each other. Someone was sitting
between them. One of the pool balls
met a corner pocket, and she didn't realize
until after she pulled out her comb and
shook her hair what she was really saying.
Earlier that evening, when it was still sunny,
they had walked the garden path. He had
opened his mouth, smiled, *Would you look
at that,* and when she confessed she needed her glasses,
he said, *Three white-tailed deer. And over there*
(he pointed at three writers they both knew)
*that's three humans with a stick.* She laughed.
If it had been a date, she might have brushed
his arm. Now here they sat, someone
between them on the sofa, not even looking
at each other when she unpinned her hair.
The clack, the strike. When the fight
broke between the two guys playing pool,
you'd think the first blow came from the sculptor
who did nothing but work and smoke dope,
but it was the bigger one who finally felt
he had been taunted enough, and when
the caretaker ran in out of nowhere to break it up,
his hat dripping rain, everyone was surprised
when he began to weep about the wife
they had thought dead, not gone.
The green felt was spattered with water,
not blood. The deer had slipped in
to a pocket of trees. This is as far
as the story may go.

## We Kept Having to Say

I don't remember what we were arguing about,
only that we were in public — in Hugo's
on a Friday night, winter as much as it can be
in Fayetteville, and in case you haven't been,
the red door to the cafe is below street level and
inside the heating pipes are red and exposed,
and the lights burn red as well. That night
it was so crowded it was hard to hear, so
we felt free to keep going while we waited
for a table — spiteful, vicious, everything
below the belt, the kind of fight where after a while
you have no idea what you have said
much less believe, only that you are trying
to stay afloat on your little raft of words
and not let the other party wipe you out.
But over the cackle of glasses and forks
we kept having to say *What? Could you
repeat that?* Even seated at a round table
too small to hold our plates and the drinks
we desperately wanted by then, it did not stop.
We sat in the red-checkered, red-lit din and let
that argument swell and thin like an inflating balloon,
our coats being knocked off our chairs by people
on their way out, and it wasn't until we asked
the waitress what we owed that she said
Nothing; a stranger had paid our bill for us
and told her not to tell us until he had gone.
All the way home in the new snow —
silent, now, abashed — we wondered
who he was, what he had heard,
whether he loved or pitied us.

## Abyss

If a good love poem requires a little darkness,
how far down can I go? Thousands of feet?
The coelacanth is near, but it's too easy —
the metaphor nettable and clear, the lost
link found, the beginnings of our own bones
in its pelvic fins — and I want to write about love

with depth to hold the unverifiable, the oarfish
that survives with half its body gone.
I want it to hold the giant squid no one has seen
alive, strong enough to scar sperm whales;
sailors have claimed its tentacles unfurl
from the night's water, taking down their mates.

But can such poems survive these confused witnesses?
Can they handle the scanty evidence that surfaces:
the mottled sick and dead, the night-feeding
viperfish impaling victims with fangs
at high speed, its first vertebra designed
to absorb the shock? And how much horror

can this poem sustain before you forbid me to say
some call this love, the hagfish that bores
into the unsuspecting body, rasping
its flesh from inside out? Am I making you
uncomfortable? The pressure at these depths
could crush a golf ball. Are you cold?

Or is it enough to be awed by the blue-
green photophores of the lantern fish, the brief
and brilliant light displays? What the lights say:
*I want you. Not so close. I am moonlight;*
*I am not here. I would eat you raw —*
tell me if you want me to stop.

## On Marriage

I like watching my husband on a ladder
sealing the bungalow windows in plastic for winter.
The task requires all his attention —
straight tracks of tape along the frames, the unzip
of the paper covers so that both sides are sticky.
I like his ease. I have been standing here
inside this window, dust cloth in hand,
and still he has not noticed me
watching the way he holds his body
three rungs from the ground — leaning his weight
on a stiffened right leg, left moccasin cocked
on the next step up, slim hips pulled in.
I like the pencil behind his ear,
the jackknife he unfolds to shear the plastic

sheet to size. How he measures it, almost
invisible, fluttering against the glass,
and his wedding band flashes gold against
the gray weather of Saint Paul, bright
like the churchbells calling this fall morning.
And do you know what he will do when at last
he sees me standing here? Mock-start, then wink,
get back to work. We have lived in this house
a few winters now and I have begun to learn
its rhythms. I know, for instance, that right now
we could barely hear each other,
if one of us decided to ask a question.

# K

The hieroglyph for the first letter of my name is *Kaph,*
meaning *palm of the hand,* meaning *give;*
in front of a word, in Arabic, *kaph* means *your.*
I am walking along the Mississippi River with a man
who is filling his hands with leaves
for the first time since he left his home
in Africa. There is no end
to the list of trees he wants named.
Let me open my hands. The Midwest's trees:
green ash, river birch, swamp white oak, silver
maple, old friends picked from a crowd.
A political prisoner once said he survived
by learning to give himself over
to the rhythms of his beatings. Head, back,
feet — each delivers a different pain.
What's in a name is the beginning of knowing:
the bur oaks' tortured branches, the tortured man.
The man holds the leaves behind his back as he walks.
*Terror* from *tremble,* the cottonwood leaves
over our heads. *Kaph* is the *hollow*, the emptied hand,
cupped palm you fill with water at the river's edge.
*Mississippi* is Ojibwe for *Father of the Waters.*
But naming is nothing like being or knowing.
*Kaph* is a hand like a spoon.
When the priest raises her hands palm-up and says
*Go in peace* I think she means, *Give*
*everything away and your hands will fill.* In Arabic,
*kaph* as a prefix means *like, as though* the flash
of gold finches in the grass of Minneapolis is the flash
of red-billed fire finches against an umbrella tree.
Add the word *for* to *kaph,* and it becomes *you.*

## She thinks of herself as a green Dodge van

lumbering down I-75 after 2 a.m., driven
by a mother. On the bench in back
Sister whispers to Brother, "She's drunk
again." And if the van is this woman, the O
of the steering wheel is her mouth in lipsticked

surprise; there's plenty of play in it. A silver goat
swings from the rearview mirror, aims its horns
at the boy and the girl in back. They were alive
when the van was built, but it's from before
they can remember, they can't imagine

it parked in front of a flower shop, a van to pass
their eyes over without noticing. The woman
is a van the children inside are ashamed of, indelicate
with rusted quarter-panels, no longer capable
of blending in. The girl's friend sits at her side.

That makes three kids with stretched-out
seat belts that don't work, if you're keeping track,
in the back of the van driven by a drunk mother
a van that is really a woman (remember?)
a woman entering the shiny headlight stream

of the universe. Earlier, the van waited
in the frosted dark of the bowling alley's parking lot,
imagining league night, the mother's vodka tonics,
kids leaning on a jukebox pulsing watery light. Scores
were being projected overhead, and shadows

of hands bigger than life were writing in spares,
X's for strikes. The bowling alley's a memory,
and the van could not get inside it. You must not
confuse her with Brother, or Sister, now crying.
You might well confuse her with the friend

gazing out the window, pretending not to know.
But the van of this woman carries them all.
You must not confuse her with the mother,
even when she confuses herself with that mother,
drunk, hurtling down the highway after 2 a.m.

## Oarlock, Oar *(Y, W, V, U, F)*

still I hail from smokestacks girders closed

factories McLouth Steel's poured slag turning the night

sky and black river orange the tight typeface of houses

in River Rouge Wyandotte the steel and auto tribes

tribe of the alphabet job shops the fathers who set

cutting tools on screw machines to make in multiples

in sixes packets of ear plugs the men made deaf shift

changes at three the line must never stop nothing could

not mothers who taught us the alphabet shapes

of oxen boats houses camels letters row on row

to prop us up row the ideas forward the spear

the snake the needle tooth *Y W V U* and *F*

all hailing from the same tribe the same hieroglyph father

*oar* or *oarlock* depending the alphabet not unlike

the world we lived in once we lived there the letters

trundled forth on their tracks boxcars shaking full

of gleaming two-doors leather seats body by Fisher

and yes I hail from unbeautiful artifice things

that made us late (barred tracks flashed lights opened

bridges) a tribe of shipbuilders iron ore taconite men

whose hands would not wash clean the machinery

and the machinery of the river the made *thing*

more important than we were the things themselves

not the idea of them I thought the letters books

a different place the books were not the way

out but in the letters embodying mirroring making what is

the oarlock what the oar still I hail from the Grosse Ile crew

team pulling on the river before school matching letter

jackets forgotten on the dock the catch release their blades

## Handwriting Analysis

On the first day of fourth grade, Mrs. Hunter
collected our penmanship samples to save

until June; by then, she said, we'd write
in the handwriting we would have all our lives.

Though she probably read that in a book
on child development, I was so excited

I could hardly stand it. In nine months
my adult self would be born, she would

send me a letter; in the ways she swooped,
careened, and crossed her *t*'s, I could

read everything I would need to know.
We were writing ourselves into the future.

We came closer each time we turned
the silver gears in the sharpener near the door,

the wood shavings tumbling inside,
smelling as if a house were being built.

## Photograph: My Parents' First Christmas

Kind of like the Pietà but set in working-class Detroit:
        my mother perches on my father's lap, her shift

celery-green, not unlike something Gidget might have worn.

My father's biceps bulge; he stares the camera down.
        She tilts her head toward the puppy stretched

across their laps. The room? Mostly empty. Console

television's gray-faced. A stiff new easy chair
        that will grow more easy through my childhood,

a tree decked out in silver, blue. You have to look

hard to see the tension in their arms
        as they push down the half-trained puppy

to hold it still. When they shamed it for failing

to be good, I bet it cringed, then shook
        an old balled-up sock of my father's in its teeth.

I bet they laughed; they wanted things to work.

## Mirror Palace

My sister and I teeter through
the kitchen, holding mirrors
beneath our noses, looking

down into the tilted ceiling
that has become our floor. It's
Saturday. Our parents play

old records. They're drinking
coffee at the table, paying
the water bill. We bump

their chairs, step gingerly
over lintels, over light
fixtures jutting from our floor.

We are flies; we walk cracks
in the plaster. We can
follow erratic, jagged roads

and find our way home.
In the console, records hover
in a stack, one by one collapse

onto the turntable. Smokey
Robinson is shopping, the
Drifters are up on the roof.

The Marvelettes say Wait
a minute, wait a minute,
and our mirrors cloud

with breath, the way
the mirror didn't
on the morning the Drifters

held it under the nose
of their lead singer. Hours
later they recorded

"Under the Boardwalk"
all the same, unable
to lose the studio time,

a backup guy stepping in
to take the lead as
Rudy Lewis stepped into

a foggy sky cracked by branches,
the world below still round,
hand-held, unreachable.

## Virginity

I knew it made me prized, helpless; that losing it
would make me bleed. Because the desires of boys
angered my father, so did I — though desire

seemed unconnected to the way they would, in a pack,
stand in a driveway and call out invitations.

If I could pass and seem unshaken,
they would shout at my back, *You bitch!*

This long afternoon on the mountain in Winslow
Ellen and I drink tea, look out her back window,
and wait for a purebred colt to be born.

The Arabian mare has lost her mucus plug,
and there will be no other sign: prey animals
have their babies fast, to walk away before the blood
attracts a predator.
                    I could not have known
my father wanted to deliver me unharmed;

I would not have trusted anyone to see

that something growing inside me wanted out,
wanted to be shaking and raw, wet and new.

## By Now the Warning Bell Has Rung and None of Us Can Drive

Mrs. Knapp has yanked the bus onto the shoulder
and thundered into her hand-held mic she has worked hard

all year, she drove in a fright wig and fake nose
on Halloween, she held a Rubik's cube contest for us

and will not drive us to the junior high until
we sing her a Christmas carol. But it's too late,

the kids in the back seats know they have her,
and when she asks for "Frosty" they sing

"Jingle Bells" and when her jolly voice splinters
one-horse open sleighs are fine, just fine,

they switch to "Deck the Halls." I'm not one of them,
I'm an oldest child, one of the many

who dot this bus. You can spot us a mile off
in dense fog. We wear the orange fluorescent

belts of the safety patrol, criss-
crossed over our chests like bandoliers.

For Mrs. Knapp I would sing, I would
do whatever she asks, if I could hear my voice

through two carols sung at once, or even
over Mrs. Knapp, who is weeping,

screaming, forget the mic, she's brandishing
the brass key to the bus but acting as if we've got it.

The kids in the back may forget all this by lunch.
Some hum the tune she wants. Others glance

at watches, press noses against dirty windows, watch
the grown-ups drive by in dress-up clothes.

We have to bide our time and hate her quietly
until the day we're old enough to seize the wheel.

## Transparent

She does not want to
wear the white blouse to school.
She is one of the only girls in her class
who wears a bra. *Would you rather the boys
saw something else?* her mother asks,
missing the point entirely. She wants
not to have a body. She wants a shirt
that gives up nothing. She wants
her mother to stop driving
her down by the river at night,
telling secrets. The Buick
is big and midnight blue, with plushy
seats and chrome detail. An aqua
digital display. Like riding in the night
sky, but darker; like fish under
the black water along one side.
The fanciest houses in town
are on the other, windows
lit yellow squares.
The people inside carry dishes
away and read and can't see them
but might agree, if they knew,
that *seeing* is not the same
as *seeing through.*

# M

The Berkshire hills the book that opens

again with each curve where the woods take back

what they just said ditch lilies ditch lilies

open orange eager in the Berkshires the mills

are no longer milling paper milling wool

they're milling memories of themselves

as useful they mill this skein of highway clumps

of lilies woolly thoughts the letter M its hieroglyph

a set of Mediterranean waves and the Phoenicians

who drew M first ship-makers wave-walkers

consider them first looking out then in        the mills

are milling the Housatonic river it skims

a thousand rocks is almost close enough to touch all

landscape here is intimate hemmed in a book

close to the face not *an open book* as we say

more the way a baby sees from its mother's breast

to her face and that is all an open book is

one small room its talk a little talk its form

a reinforcement of five hundred years of private

thought along with the invention of the separate

room a sudden set of separate fires the ancient

Berkshire hills their mills are milling spotted

dairy cows and woolly sheep alphabet of camels

oxen fish if my northern tribe had drawn M first

M would have been a hieroglyph for *milk* the cows

goats sheep they learned to drink from or starve

*la mer, la mère* the sound of M for *mother*

in nearly every language the early sounds a baby

makes M for delicious the motor's hum delicious

drowsing off the shape of these worn-down hills the mills

mill poems walls of stone tonight they mill the stars

M for *ma*, the Japanese idea of space

and silence as a thing not absence on the radio

today they talk about the death of books

of spacious thought the book a footnote

a single clump of lilies one river thread

I think of books as milk from other animals

## O, P, R, S (Eye/Mouth/Head/Tongue)

At dusk the deer appear on the highway shoulder,
more of them as the light continues to die.
Suddenly they simply *are*,
bare brown outlines, hesitant. I am
to scan for movement, eye-shine; my husband,
to brake when I say *deer*. If I say *deer*
*are the world at dusk, barred owls* — if antlers
are trees in silhouette; if as the light goes down
we are coming out of our hiding places, on the move
to night feeding grounds, hunted, haunted,
should I say I see these things,
even if I cannot name the pine
the deer walk among, could not track
their hoof prints to the river. If the ribbon
my life moves along is thin: *diner,*
*asphalt.* The poem is older than
ochre, sienna horses inked on stone,
older than my body, can I say it?
*The deer are the world at dusk.*
My body cannot help but remember.
The deer cannot help bolting into the road
in front of our car. They cannot help walking
with the name we gave them
which once did not mean *deer*
but any untamed thing that breathes
and traces back to the Sanskrit for *he perishes.*

# Q

In the Phoenician alphabet *Q* is *qoph*,

     meaning *monkey*. In Hebrew, *qoph* means

   *eye of the needle*. Meaning, *Impossible*.

Meaning, *Unthinkable*. Art is about the big *q's*:

     *quest, quirky, quixotic, quench.*

   Magical Q, fifth element of the Greeks,

moonstuff that sleeps inside us all, *quintessence.*

     Like *bioluminescence*. Effusive Q: the Milky Way

   of Queen Anne's lace along the road, the *quartz*

geode that resolves into a cave of diamonds

     when raised to the eye. The *quotidian*

   made rare, monkey-minded Q viewed from the back,

its tail poised, ready to swing. The love/

     hate of impossible passion, *Q,* and the way

   a man fits into a woman makes me believe in

the old gods, their lightning bolts

     and whims, the needle's jealous flash and prick —

   the gods plucking our strings, playing us.

When the woman in the Song

        of Solomon says: *Open a door for me as big*

     *as a needle's eye, and I will open a door for you*

*through which may enter tents and camels,*

       she means *Q*—love as the silken tent,

    all honey and figs, all on the *q.t.,*

the bloody feet of angels and their dervish

       on the pin. If *P* is for *passion,* from the Latin

    to *suffer,* then *Q* is for *quarantine,*

the trying-to-get-over, the bitter

       home-brewed cure—*Quacksalver,*

    not *quicksilver,* not the broken thermometer,

not life that runs through my fingers

       shining. Q for *to quail,* Q for *quaint,*

    which once meant *skillfully made.* As in, *I am*

*fearfully and wonderfully made. Q* as in *quash,*

       from the French *to crack,* there's no use

crying over broken eggs. This afternoon in Paris

strung along the *quais*, the booksellers' stalls

are shining after rain. They're selling

odd game pieces I want to buy. Mah-jongg tiles,

Scrabble tiles. In the *Qu'ran* it is written (meaning

*Q; meaning, O pure-hearted readers, O*

*Katrina, don't be fools): They do not show a man a palm*

*tree of gold, nor an elephant going through the eye of a needle—*

## I think of myself as the old borrowed bicycle

ridden by the young woman — nearly a girl —

on her way to New England Medical.
She grips the handlebar and wilting cosmos

all at once. The girl who, that morning, drank coffee
by the woodstove at the housing cooperative.

The girl who does not cooperate. I am not
a metaphor, just vehicle. Am driven

defensively, reflect after dark, navigate
blaring streets. The girl could be the metaphor's

other half, but isn't neat, for one thing. Showers
too often and too long, does not phrase her troubles

in *I* statements at house meetings. She's a guest
in this triple decker, its basement full of used bicycles

on their way to Nicaragua. Life to come,
for the bicycles: a constant weaving

past flaming fields and churches, pistols cocked
at many boys younger than the comatose man

she visits in ICU. The girl drinks her coffee,
stands at the window on the top floor,

the quilt of orchards beyond Roxbury unfolding
into a future where people will always be missing.

Her job is to be carried, to remember
this fall forever. My job is to bear the girl.

## Earthworms

It is raining again this morning. I remember
it rained then, too, that summer morning
we lay crosswise on the bed, the curtains
grazing our heads, quickened
by the damp wind. Outside, the earth
was opening and the worms had surfaced,
blind. They have eaten every bit of dirt
that makes our yard. In bed
at night, we turn the story
of the child whose heart we never heard,
the child who never heard rain. And we don't
care, we let it surface — we open
ourselves, from time to time, to happiness.

# X

I promise to solve for X. I promise I will write
a poem about forgiveness. Even if it is April
and another college boy has drowned in the Midwest.
XX means "girl," XY means "boy." A serial killer,
some say. Others: The boys are drunk
and we have rivers. We also have rails,
trestles in fields of corn, steel mills.
A restless moon, a horizon you can see clear to,
crows on telephone poles like Xs strung together.
As unfertilized eggs we all begin as XXs.
Even if we have lost dozens
in the Mississippi, eight in LaCrosse
alone, this poem is about forgiveness. It tries
to solve for X—X the cross, X the Christ, X
to X things out. The boy in Saint Cloud. The boy
at Saint John's, where the monks bake bread
and copy the Bible by hand. When the moon
is dark and new. X the unknown,
X for *times*. X for ten,
for more than ten. On the Web site's map,
the gravestones marked with little crosses
pop up along I-94 like crocuses, until you can't see one
for another. It is Easter. The red-winged blackbirds
are coming back to Minnesota, their wings' tips
feather the river along. The river
is a swish of calligrapher's ink,
the boys are drowning inside the X—
X for the stranger, Mr. X. I love the Mississippi,
how it can mirror back the world without us in it.
How it keeps insisting to the bluffs, *Sandstone—*
*river—limestone—river—shale—river—river.*
The river of thoughts about Mr. X has worn through
us almost that long. XO, I kiss you,
the letter is sealed. I do not want to die
without lifting a child of my own from the water.

## Plums

Doctor Williams you live in the house with your poems

you wash your hands when it grows too dark to write

you step into the yard past the wheelbarrow

bits of broken green bottle glass shining the girls

of New Jersey we gorge ourselves on plums

we draw the latch-string on the door of sense in the clouds

you ask the branches to rain down the plums

you ask the branches to rain down the babies

you tell us the babies are plums

Doctor Williams in your house you wash your hands

after delivering babies you write poems when it grows dark

in the orchard we girls of New Jersey eat plums

we suck bite and spit out the flesh-threaded stones

we shut the door to the news it is difficult to get from poems

you say branches shake furious girls hold out your aprons

you hold your palms to the sky and say trees

rustle your heart-shaped leaves girls gather your children

Doctor Williams you write your wheelbarrow songs

step into the yard past the shining bits of bottle glass

say rock-a-bye boughs break Making is a woman in blue

bring her paper to sketch the plum blossoms shaking

erasing the sky we must fill with plums poems babies

in New Jersey we eat cold plums all night dust off

the white bloom run our thumbs along clefts

we gorge ourselves on the falling plums we glut

and we slurp from your window Doctor Williams

you loose branches loose the stars the green

broken bottle glass shines you dandle babies stack

alphabet blocks say a fine one yes ma'am! our Making

is a woman in blue who holds out her skirts

she wipes clean the paper trees sky our sticky hands

fills our sky-colored aprons again and again

## Z Ghazal

The author should say something has changed by the end.
What if Z hasn't always been the alphabet's end?

*Zayin,* ⌶, was the seventh sign, and it meant *manacle.*
The Phoenicians changed it to *weapon.* Enemies met their ends.

The stars threw down their spears. One of the hunters
had bad aim. Now *Z* is a wandering path, not the end.

The ball of yarn unwinds ahead of the hermits
pacing the labyrinth's alleys. You can't, in the end,

close the book—not on *zany,* not on the heart, on *zydeco,*
*zenith,* the *ghazal.* Not on the zygote's math, Zen's end-

less *now* and *now.* Not on the zipper's sudden revelations.
Not on who you are. There's no new stripes on a zebra's end,

and to leave your childhood sandpit, you must hoist
yourself out on unconnected rungs. The alphabet used to end

with &, old Z—you lightning bolt, you jazzy sloe gin dizz,
you Batmobile of *Zonk!* and *Zap!*—here your razzle-dazzle fizzles

but not the long trudge home. Life's a zoo; our life's work, prying
open its bars, unleashing the zodiac from its cages. In the end

we forge pure silver spears, and Katrina makes peace with nothing.
What will protect us? The words will be our weapons. In the end.

# Notes

In "A Ghazal," lines from the poem "A" are from *The Hangman's Lament: Poems*, a collection of poems by the Danish poet Henrik Nordbrandt, translated by Thom Satterlee (Green Integer Press, 2003).

"Self-Portrait in 1970" was inspired by David Roderick's self-portrait poems in *Blue Colonial*.

"C Ghazal" quotes T. S. Eliot's poem "The Journey of the Magi."

The phrase "courage and horror stand side by side" is from a speech given by Doug Johnson, Director of the Center for Victims of Torture, at the 10.1.07 production of *Speak Truth to Power* at the Minneapolis Children's Theater.

The Phoenician symbol used to open the third section of the book is *lamedh* or ᠘, meaning "goad/prod," and became the letter L.

Poems constructed like "Oarlock, Oar," "M," and "N" were inspired by the poems of Leslie Harrison, and are for her; although "Oarlock, Oar" was not written for writer and editor Jeanne Leiby, I offer it in her memory.

"On the Bog Road" is after Pablo Neruda's "Poetry." "Fuchsia" owes a debt to "Deora De" by Ethna McKiernan.

The symbol used to open the final section is *teth* or ⊗, meaning "good"; this symbol disappeared before the creation of the Latin alphabet.

"X" was written for Deborah Keenan.

"Z Ghazal" was written for Jim Cihlar.

I am indebted to many books, people, and institutions, but especially Thomas Cahill's *How the Irish Saved Civilization* (Anchor, 1996); the team working on the Saint John's Bible, the first to be done by hand since the invention of movable type; and the Hill Museum and Manuscript Library at Saint John's College, Collegeville, MN.

**Katrina Vandenberg** is the author of *Atlas* and co-author of a chapbook, *On Marriage.* Her poetry and nonfiction have appeared in *The Southern Review, The American Scholar, Orion, Post Road, Poets and Writers,* and other magazines. She has received fellowships from the McKnight, Bush, and Fulbright Foundations; been a Tennessee Williams Scholar at the Sewanee Writers' Conference; and held residencies at the Amy Clampitt House, the Poetry Center of Chicago, and the MacDowell Colony. She teaches in The Creative Writing Programs at Hamline University in Saint Paul, Minnesota, and lives four blocks from campus with her husband, novelist John Reimringer, and their daughter Anna.

**More Poetry from Milkweed Editions**

To order books or for more information, contact Milkweed at
(800) 520-6455
or visit our Web site
(www.milkweed.org).

*A Hotel Lobby at the Edge of the World*
By Adam Clay

*Gaze*
By Christopher Howell

*The City, Our City*
By Wayne Miller

*What have you done to our ears to make us hear echoes?*
By Arlene Kim

*The Nine Senses*
By Melissa Kwasny

*Sharks in the Rivers*
By Ada Limón

**Milkweed Editions**

Founded as a nonprofit organization in 1980, Milkweed Editions is an independent publisher. Our mission is to identify, nurture and publish transformative literature, and build an engaged community around it.

**Join Us**

In addition to revenue generated by the sales of books we publish, Milkweed Editions depends on the generosity of institutions and individuals like you. In an increasingly consolidated and bottom-line-driven publishing world, your support allows us to select and publish books on the basis of their literary quality and transformative potential. Please visit our Web site (www.milkweed. org) or contact us at (800) 520-6455 to learn more.

**Milkweed Editions,** a nonprofit publisher, gratefully acknowledges sustaining support from the following:

Maurice and Sally Blanks
Emilie and Henry Buchwald
The Bush Foundation
The Patrick and Aimee Butler
    Foundation
Timothy and Tara Clark
Betsy and Edward Cussler
The Dougherty Family Foundation
Julie B. DuBois
John and Joanne Gordon
Ellen Grace
William and Jeanne Grandy
John and Andrea Gulla
the Jerome Foundation
The Lerner Foundation
The Lindquist & Vennum Foundation
Sanders and Tasha Marvin
The McKnight Foundation
Mid-Continent Engineering
The Minnesota State Arts Board,
    through an appropriation by
    the Minnesota State Legislature
    and a grant from the National
    Endowment for the Arts
Kelly Morrison and John Willoughby
The National Endowment for the Arts
The Navarre Corporation
Ann and Doug Ness
Jörg and Angie Pierach

The RBC Foundation USA
Pete Rainey
Deborah Reynolds
Cheryl Ryland
Schele and Philip Smith
The Target Foundation
The Travelers Foundation
Moira and John Turner
Edward and Jenny Wahl

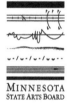

Interior design and typesetting by Hopkins/Baumann
Typeset in Bodoni Book with Bodoni Bold
Printed on acid-free 30% postconsumer-waste paper
by Edwards Brothers, Inc.